SandCastle
Let's Go!

LET'S GO
BY
HOT AIR BALLOON

ANDERS HANSON

Consulting Editor, Diane Craig, M.A./Reading Specialist

ABDO Publishing Company

Published by ABDO Publishing Company, 8000 West 78th Street, Edina, MN 55439.

Printed in the United States.

Editor: Pam Price
Curriculum Coordinator: Nancy Tuminelly
Cover and Interior Design and Production: Mighty Media
Photo Credits: iStockphoto (Eileen Hart, Karen Locke), Shutterstock

Library of Congress Cataloging-in-Publication Data

Hanson, Anders, 1980-

   Let's go by hot air balloon / Anders Hanson.
     p. cm. -- (Let's go!)
   ISBN 978-1-59928-899-4
   1. Hot air balloons--Juvenile literature. 2. Ballooning--Juvenile literature. I. Title.

   TL638.H36 2008
   629.133'22--dc22

                                           2007012584

SandCastle™ Level: Transitional

SandCastle™ books are created by a team of professional educators, reading specialists, and content developers around five essential components—phonemic awareness, phonics, vocabulary, text comprehension, and fluency—to assist young readers as they develop reading skills and increase their general knowledge. All books are written, reviewed, and leveled for guided reading, early intervention reading, and Accelerated Reader® programs for use in shared, guided, and independent reading and writing activities to support a balanced approach to literacy instruction. The SandCastle™ series has four levels that correspond to early literacy development. The levels are provided to help teachers and parents select appropriate books for young readers.

Emerging Readers
(no flags)

Beginning Readers
(1 flag)

Transitional Readers
(2 flags)

Fluent Readers
(3 flags)

SandCastle™ would like to hear from you. Please send us your comments or questions.

sandcastle@abdopublishing.com

Hot air balloons
float in the air.
They are used
mostly for short,
fun rides.

A large fan fills the envelope with air.

A burner heats the air inside the balloon.

Because hot air rises, the balloon rises too.

People ride in the basket.

Ron watches the balloon take off. He sits on his dad's shoulders.

The yellow balloon is shaped like the sun. The blue balloon is shaped like an octopus.

Ann and James got married in a hot air balloon. They will take a balloon ride after the wedding.

The flower-shaped
hot air balloon is
Mary's favorite!

HAVE YOU BEEN
IN A HOT AIR BALLOON?

WHERE DID YOU GO?

PARTS OF A HOT AIR BALLOON

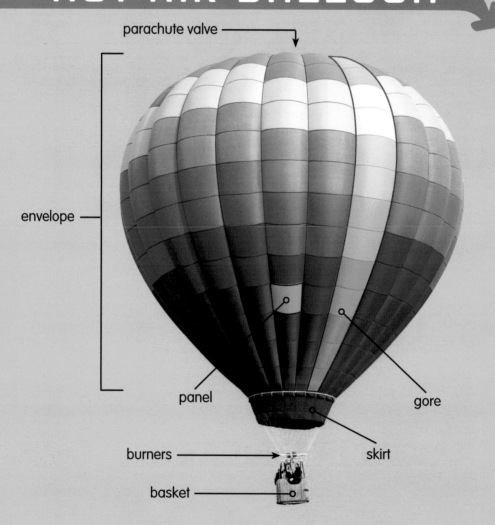

parachute valve

envelope

panel

gore

burners

skirt

basket

FAST FACTS

The fabric that makes up the balloon is called the envelope.

A sheep, a duck, and a rooster were the first hot air balloon passengers in 1783.

The first complete trip around the world in a hot air balloon happened in 1999.

GLOSSARY

burner – a device in which fuel is burned.

fabric – cloth.

favorite – someone or something that you like best.

passenger – a person riding in a vehicle.

shoulder – the part of the body between the upper arm and the neck.

wedding – a marriage ceremony.

To see a complete list of SandCastle™ books and other nonfiction titles from ABDO Publishing Company, visit **www.abdopublishing.com**.

8000 West 78th Street, Edina, MN 55439 • 800-800-1312 • 952-831-1632 fax